THE REAL SCIENCE OF
SUPERSPEED
AND
SUPERSTRENGTH

Christina Hill

Lerner Publications ◆ Minneap

T0018747

Lerner Publications Company
An imprint of Lerner Publishing Group, Inc.
241 First Avenue North
Minneapolis, MN 55401 USA

For reading levels and more information, look up this title at www.lernerbooks.com.

Library of Congress Cataloging-in-Publication Data
Names: Hill, Christina, author.
Title: The real science of superspeed and superstrength / Christina Hill.
Description: Minneapolis : Lerner Publications, [2022] | Series: The real science of superpowers (Alternator books) | Includes bibliographical references and index. | Audience: Ages 8–12 | Audience: Grades 4–6 | Summary: "Whoosh! Superheroes can run faster than any vehicle can carry them. See how scientists and engineers use technology to help people move and work like never before"— Provided by publisher.
Identifiers: LCCN 2021021710 (print) | LCCN 2021021711 (ebook) | ISBN 9781728441238 (library binding) | ISBN 9781728449593 (paperback) | ISBN 9781728445328 (ebook)
Subjects: LCSH: Speed—Juvenile literature. | Force and energy—Juvenile literature. | Superheroes—Juvenile literature. | Technological innovations—Juvenile literature.
Classification: LCC Q175.2 .H55 2022 (print) | LCC Q175.2 (ebook) | DDC 531/.112—dc23

LC record available at https://lccn.loc.gov/2021021710
LC ebook record available at https://lccn.loc.gov/2021021711

Manufactured in the United States of America
1-49894-49737-7/7/2021

STRONG AND SPEEDY

Dogs don't look left and right when they cross the road. Good thing there are heroes to save them!

"**S**omebody save my dog!" You hear cries for help and see a crowd gathering. Two blocks away, a curious puppy is running through a traffic-filled city street. With a burst of superspeed, you race toward the puppy, reaching him in less than a second. But before you can grab him, a horn blares a warning. You glance up and see a huge truck zooming right toward you!

Luckily, your superpowers don't stop at speed. You also have superstrength! With no effort, you pick up the puppy with one hand while your other hand stretches out and brings the truck to a gentle halt.

With superspeed and superstrength, you could save all the wandering puppies in the world! Sounds like a dream, right? But what would it really mean to have these powers?

Superstrength is a common superpower for comic book heroes.

Superspeed is a super ability!

Many comic book and movie heroes are naturally superfast. Others need magical items to assist them, like special suits, magic hammers, or jets. Plenty of characters can travel faster than the speed of sound, which is 761 miles (1,225 km) per hour. Some are famous for being faster than a speeding bullet, or about 1,800 miles (2,897 km) per hour. A few can even move at, or surpass, the speed of light!

What about traveling at light speed in real life? According to physicist Albert Einstein, anything with mass will never be able to travel as fast as light. Mass is the measure of weight, or the amount of stuff an object is made of. Light is made up of photons, which are particles without mass. They don't need energy to move. Light travels 186,282 miles (299,792 km) per second. Humans have mass, so according to the known laws of physics, we will never be able to travel at the speed of light.

Shock waves make a cone of pressurized air. As the air spreads out, it creates a loud noise called a sonic boom.

SUPERFAST FACT

...ure waves build when something ...els through air faster than the speed ...und. This creates a shock wave. *BOOM!*

Let's look at the science behind superspeed. Two things rubbing against each other cause friction. Friction causes heat. More speed means more rubbing, which means more heat. If humans ran at superspeed, the friction of their feet rubbing on the ground would build enough heat to burn skin. Regular shoes wouldn't stand a chance. Also, think about what happens to your head and neck when you are in a car that jerks forward suddenly. Superspeed acceleration would need to be gradual enough that the human body could survive it.

Striking a match causes enough friction to start a fire.

Another thing to consider is the presence of particles in the air. While air may look empty, it is not. At superspeed, tiny dust particles would cut through human skin. Items falling to Earth from space burn because of the friction caused by rubbing against air molecules in Earth's atmosphere at high speeds. Spacecraft returning to Earth are fitted with special shields to push heat from friction outward as they land.

High-tech suits and shoes could help protect people at superspeeds, but reaction time is another issue. It takes the brain one-sixth to one-third of a second to react to something we see. At normal speeds, reaction time isn't too much of a problem. If you are running down the street and you see a tree branch ahead, you have enough time to duck. But the faster you go, the less reaction time you have. That tree branch could be lethal. Even running through an empty desert could be dangerous. A tiny bug could cause serious damage if you hit it head-on.

Moving slowly gives us enough reaction time to avoid obstacles.

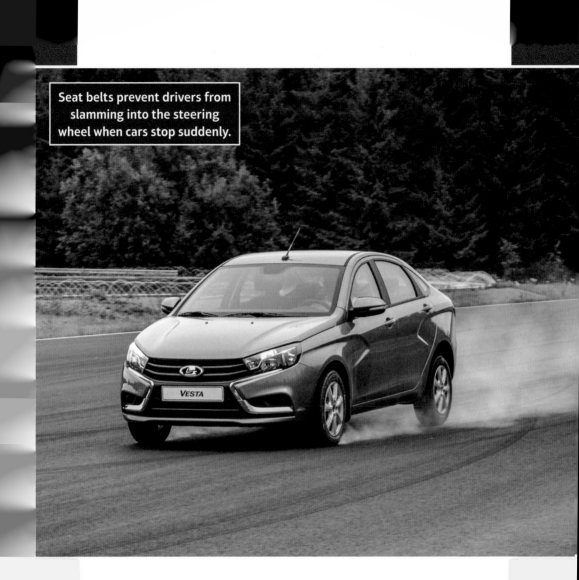

Seat belts prevent drivers from slamming into the steering wheel when cars stop suddenly.

Even if a human could overcome the problem of reaction time, they would need to slow their speed at a safe rate. Have you ever been in a car that had to swerve or brake suddenly? If you had to stop suddenly from a superfast speed, that feeling would be multiplied, and your body would not survive.

Think of all the things you could do with superstrength.

Some fictional heroes are so strong that they can lift trucks with one hand or stop speeding trains with their bodies. How did they get superstrength? For nonhuman characters from different planets, their powers might be part of their genetic makeup. Others gain strength through magic spells, genetic mutations caused by experiments, or even venom from spider bites!

AMAZING ANIMAL POWER

Think about the strongest animal on Earth. Did you imagine an elephant or a gorilla? Size doesn't always equal strength. The strongest animal is the tiny dung beetle! This mighty insect has the most strength compared to its size. It can carry 1,141 times its body weight. For the average person, that much weight would equal thirteen African elephants!

Dung beetles are the superstrong heroes of the bug world!

Most people cannot use more than fifty percent of their total strength at one time. If they learned to use 100 percent, could they be as strong as the heroes in comic books and movies? Let's look at the science behind strength.

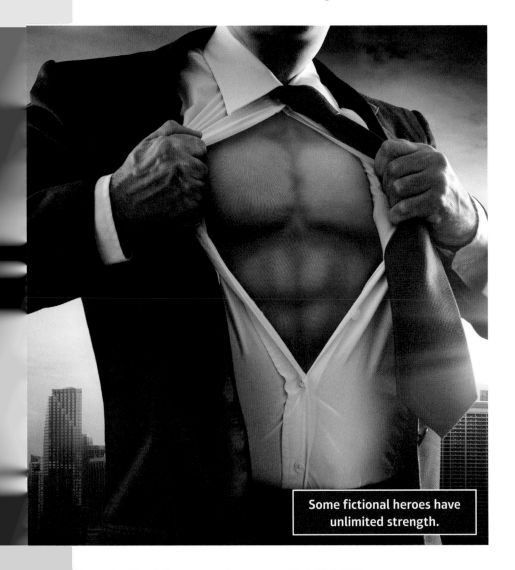

Some fictional heroes have unlimited strength.

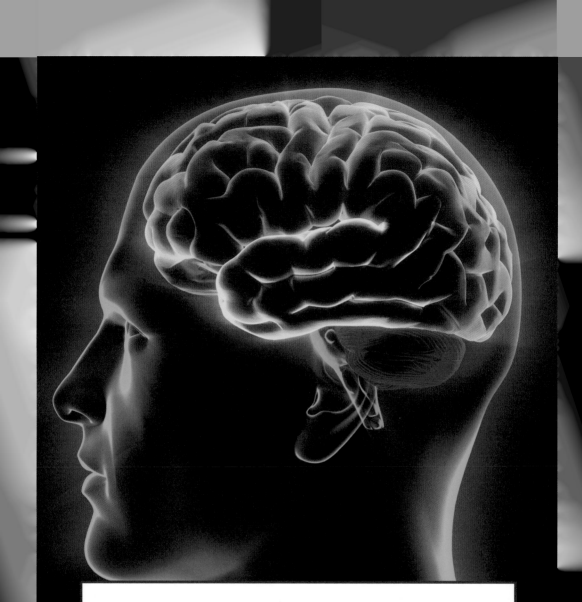

   The human brain limits how much strength we can use to prevent damage to our muscles and other body parts. Humans are smart! Our brains are designed to protect our bodies from harm—even harm caused by lifting something that is too heavy. If we used every bit of our strength to lift extremely heavy things, our bones and muscles might not be strong enough to hold them up without being damaged.

Comic book heroes usually have big muscles to show how strong they are.

Size doesn't always equal strength, but most fictional heroes have huge bodies and muscles. They can lift a car into the air—but they might struggle to squeeze behind the steering wheel!

Superstrength would make everyday tasks difficult. You could easily break your controller in half when playing video games. The sidewalk might crumble under the force of your footsteps. And being superstrong wouldn't mean you were indestructible. With superstrength, you could pick up a giant tree without straining your muscles. But a tiny splinter of wood from the tree could puncture your skin!

SUPERFAST FACT

The strongest muscles for their size in the human body are the masseters. They close our jaw when we chew.

CHAPTER 3
REAL-LIFE SUPERSPEED AND SUPERSTRENGTH

Food is fuel! We need to eat if we want to move.

Average people may not have superpowers, but they can focus on getting faster and stronger. Good nutrition is a key component. We can't grow new muscle without the right fuel, and that fuel comes from protein, nutrients, and other substances in food. Actors who play heroes in movies and on TV follow specialized diets to help them bulk up. To get bigger, they need to consume more calories than they burn while working out. A person needs to add 3,500 calories to their diet to gain 1 pound (0.5 kg) of muscle.

Super-speedy heroes probably have big appetites. Running at superspeed would burn 600 billion calories. To regain those calories, they'd have to eat 200 million slices of pizza!

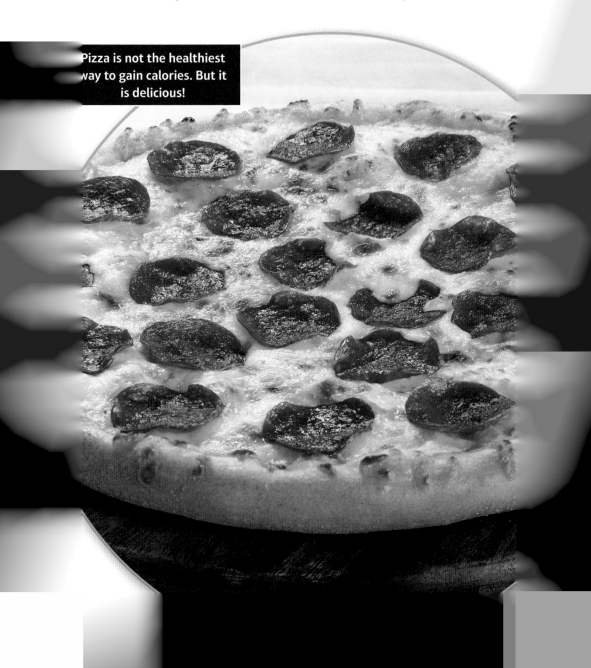

Pizza is not the healthiest way to gain calories. But it is delicious!

Just like heroes, some humans are extremely strong and fast. But many focus on being one or the other. Not all muscle is the same. Bodybuilders tend to have big, bulky muscles that help them lift weights. Runners usually have long, lean muscles that help them run long distances.

Bodybuilders target specific muscle groups as they work out.

Humans have a substance in their bodies called myostatin that limits muscle size. But some people naturally have low amounts of myostatin. Their bodies grow muscle easily and have little body fat.

SUPERFAST FACT

Bananas are the perfect body fuel! They are rich in potassium and carbohydrates, which boost energy and help muscles grow.

People only use a small amount of their potential strength and speed. But sometimes emergencies create extraordinary circumstances. Ordinary people have had moments of superstrength. In one news story, two teenage girls lifted a tractor off of their father. How is this possible? Adrenaline.

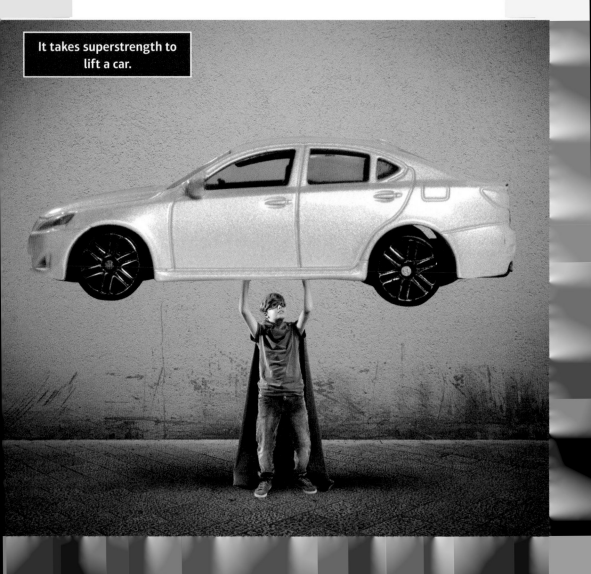

It takes superstrength to lift a car.

Adrenaline is a chemical that increases blood flow to our muscles. When our bodies are emotionally stressed, like during moments of extreme excitement or fear, adrenaline gives our muscles a boost of power! Unfortunately, scientists can't study these superstrength moments. Humans need to be in extreme situations to receive such super bursts of adrenaline. Those conditions are hard to create in a lab.

SHATTERING RECORDS

Heroes can overcome the body's limitations and reach incredible speeds.

Limitations to our physical bodies prevent us from attaining superstrength and superspeed. But scientists and engineers are working on bypassing those limitations.

The current record for human running speed is 27 miles (43 km) per hour. Since we run on two legs, scientists think our highest potential speed is not much faster. Cheetahs can run 70 miles (113 km) per hour. They always have two of their four legs exerting force on the ground. Faster speeds come from more ground time. That's why ice skating is faster than running, even if your legs move more slowly.

Cheetahs are the fastest land animal.

Even if we could overcome the problem of running on two legs, humans would still lack the energy and endurance to achieve and maintain superspeed. A powered backpack might be the burst we need! An engineering student designed a backpack with fans. Then scientists streamlined the backpack and reduced its weight. The backpack's instant acceleration allows people to run faster than they normally could.

Powered backpacks can help people move superfast on the ground or zoom through the air.

Guardian XO allows people to experience superstrength.

SUPER STEM BREAKTHROUGH

Guardian XO is a full-body exoskeleton, or robotic suit, designed for humans. The suit is comfortable and lightweight. Like an action hero, the operator can lift 200 pounds (91 kg) with ease. Companies might give these suits to employees who need to lift heavy objects. The suits would allow employees of all ages and abilities to work side by side.

Athletes are always looking to shatter strength and speed records and join the ranks of the comic book heroes. Good nutrition, exercise programs, and natural talent can only get humans so far. But with the help of science and technology, superspeed and superstrength may be in our future.

SUPER YOU!

Grab a sheet of paper, a rubber band, and a book. Then turn the flimsy sheet of paper into a superstrong hero.

You probably think you can't hold the weight of a book with one sheet of paper. But let's give the paper superstrength and see what happens. Roll the paper lengthwise into the shape of a cylinder. Use a rubber band to secure it. Stand the paper cylinder up on a tabletop and balance the book on top. Did the paper hold the book's weight?

adrenaline: a substance that increases blood flow to muscles

calories: units of heat used to show the amount of energy that foods will produce in the human body

endurance: the ability to do something difficult for a long time

engineer: a person who designs and builds machines

friction: rubbing one thing against another

pressure: the weight or force that is produced when something pushes against something else

protein: a substance found in foods such as meat, milk, eggs, and beans that is an important part of the human diet

surface area: the amount of area covered by the surface of something

LEARN MORE

Ducksters–Speed and Velocity
https://www.ducksters.com/science/physics
/speed_and_velocity.php

Hoena, Blake. *Super Speed*. Minneapolis: Bellwether Media, 2021.

Mattern, Joanne. *Super Strength*. South Egremont, MA: Red Chair Press, 2019.

Olson, Gillia M. *Muscles and Bones (A Repulsive Augmented Reality Experience)*. Minneapolis: Lerner Publications, 2021.

Polinsky, Paige V. *Super Strength*. Minneapolis: Bellwether Media, 2021.

TEDEd: If Superpowers Were Real–Super Speed
https://ed.ted.com/lessons/if-superpowers-were-real
-super-speed-joy-lin

TEDEd: If Superpowers Were Real–Super Strength
https://ed.ted.com/lessons/if-superpowers-were-real-super
-strength-joy-lin

12 Marvel and DC Super Hero Tech That Has Actually Been Invented
https://interestingengineering.com/12-marvel-and-dc-super-hero
-tech-that-has-actually-been-invented

Index

Photo Acknowledgments

Image credits: Nataba/Getty Images, p.4; RichVintage/Getty Images, p.5; Claudio Lucca/Shutterstock, p.6; yenwen/Getty Images, p.7; TheCrimsonMonkey/ Getty Images, p.8; Marc Ward/Shutterstock, p.9; Ippei Naoi/Getty Images, p.10; Yauhen_D/Shutterstock, p.11; claylib/Getty Images, p.12; RainervonBrandis/ Getty Images, p.13; RomoloTavani/Getty Images, p.14; Matthias Kulka/Getty Images, p.15; VasjaKoman/Getty Images, p.16; myboxpra/Getty Images, p.17; Alex Tihonovs/Shutterstock, p.18; Lew Robertson/Getty Images, p.19; Matthew Leete/Getty Images, p.20; Jose Luis Pelaez Inc/Getty Images, p.21; alphaspirit. it/Shutterstock, p.22; Graiki/Getty Images, 23; SerrNovik/Getty Images, p.24; Science Photo Library - MARK GARLICK/Getty Images, p.25; Theresa Martinez/ Shutterstock, p.26; JAMES ATOA/UPI/Newscom, p.27; Michael Steele/Staff/Getty Images, p.28; LIgorko/Getty Images, p.29;

Cover: SerrNovik/Getty Images